The Making of a

A Football All-Pro

All-Pro

Heinemann Library
Chicago, Illinois

Scott Ingram

© 2005 Heinemann Library
a division of Reed Elsevier Inc.
Chicago, Illinois

Customer Service   888–454–2279
Visit our website at www.heinemannlibrary.com

Edited by Geoff Barker, Rebecca Hunter and Jennifer Huston
Designed by Ian Winton
Illustrations by Peter Bull and Stefan Chabluk
Picture research by Tom Humphrey and Rachel Tisdale
Originated by Ambassador Litho Ltd
Printed in China by WKT Company Limited.

09 08 07 06 05
10 9 8 7 6 5 4 3 2 1

Library of Congress Cataloging-in-Publication Data

Ingram, Scott (William Scott)
 A football all-pro / William Scott Ingram.
     p. cm. -- (The making of a champion)
Includes bibliographical references and index.
 ISBN 1-4034-5364-0 (lib. bdg) -- ISBN 1-4034-5548-1 (pbk.)
1. Football--Juvenile literature. 2. Football players--Juvenile literature.
3. Professional sports--Juvenile literature. I. Title. II. Series.
 GV950.7.I54 2004
 796.332--dc22
                         2004003870

Acknowledgments

The author and publisher are grateful to the following for permission to reproduce copyright material:

p.4 Empics; p.5 Bettman/Corbis; p.6 Oscar White/Corbis; p.7 & 8 Bettman/Corbis; p.9 top Danny Moloshok/Getty Images; p. 9 bottom Bettman/Corbis; p. 10 Hank Walker/Getty Images; p.11 top Doug Pensinger/Getty Images; p. 11 bottom Robert Galbraith/Corbis; p. 12 Scott Nelson/Getty Images; p. 13 Otto Greule/Getty Images; p.14 & 16 Empics; p.17 Reuters/Corbis; p.18 Ronald Martinez/Getty Images; p.19 both Empics; p.20 Tom Pidgeon/Getty Images; p.21 top Bettman/Corbis; p.21 bottom Matt Stroshane/Getty Images; p.22 Empics; p.23 Rick Steward/Getty Images; p.24 Empics; p.25 Doug Pensinger/Getty Images; p.26 Brian Bahr/Getty Images; p.27 Reuters/Corbis; p.28 top Rick Stewart/Getty Images; p.28 bottom Andy Lyons/Getty Images; p.30 Matt Brown/Newsport/Corbis;31 Reuters/Corbis; p.32 Stephen Dunn/Getty Images; p.33 top Doug Pensinger/Getty Images; p.33 bottom Time Life Pictures/Getty Images; p. 34 Hunter Martin/Corbis; p. 35 top Empics; p.35 bottom Ezra Shaw/Getty Images; p. 37 bottom Wally McNamee/Corbis; p.38 Paul A. Sanders/Corbis; p.39 Brad Mangin/Corbis; p.40 Kevin Fleming/Corbis; p.41 top Bill Eppridge/Getty Images; p.41 bottom Steve Boyle/Corbis; p.42 Joe Traver/Corbis; p.43 Bettman/Corbis.

Cover photograph reproduced with permission of Jessica Rinaldi/Stringer/Reuters/Corbis.

Contents

Introduction: Super Bowl

Less than two minutes remained in Super Bowl XXXVI between the New England Patriots and the St. Louis Rams. With the score tied at 17, quarterback Tom Brady drove the Patriots from their own 20-yard line to the Ram 36-yard line. During the drive, Brady connected with Troy Brown on a key 23-yard pass play that brought the Patriots to the Ram 36-yard line. Finally, with 7 seconds remaining in the game, kicker Adam Vinatieri kicked a 48-yard field goal to give New England its first Super Bowl win. The Patriot victory, on February 3, 2002, was one of the few times in Super Bowl history that the game had been won on the final play.

Battleground

Since Super Bowl I in 1967, the annual championship game of the National Football League (NFL) has become the most popular sporting event in the country. More than a game, football resembles a battle between two opposing armies of armored people who collide violently

Kicker Adam Vinatieri (4) of the New England Patriots keeps his eyes focused on the football as he prepares to kick the game-winning field goal against the St. Louis Rams in Super Bowl XXXVI.

in an attempt to move a ball—or prevent its movement—down a playing field.

In the past century, football has achieved a unique place in society. Playing, watching, and cheering at football games, from children's leagues through high school and college, are annual fall traditions. While professional football is played by large, fast, and powerful athletes, the game itself—running, passing, kicking, tackling, and blocking—can be played by young people. Anyone who wants to work hard can be part of a team and enjoy football.

Super Bowl attendance fact

The Super Bowl attendance record is 103,985 people for Super Bowl XIV, between the Pittsburgh Steelers and the Los Angeles Rams at the Rose Bowl in Pasadena, California, on January 20, 1980.

The first football bowl

Most football games at the college or professional level are played in stadiums—either outdoors or in domes. Yet the term "bowl" is commonly used to describe football games. That's because the very first big football facility was actually a gigantic bowl—the Yale Bowl in New Haven, Connecticut. In the early 1900s, while professional football was largely unknown, college football drew enormous crowds. As a result, Yale University built the 70,000-seat, bowl-shaped facility in 1913 to meet the demand of its football fans.

The beginnings of football

The roots of football are in soccer and rugby, two sports that began in Britain during the 1820s. When rugby arrived in the United States, a form of it was adapted by colleges and universities. During the 1840s, a game called *Ballown* was played. It was little more than brawls, with dozens of players on each side using feet and fists to advance a round leather ball over an opponent's goal line. At Harvard University in Cambridge, Massachusetts, freshman and sophomore classes played a ballown-type game on the first Monday of each school year. This event became known as Bloody Monday.

First game

On November 6, 1869, Princeton University in Princeton, New Jersey, played nearby Rutgers College in what is generally considered the first real football game. Early football had little resemblance to today's game. The first games used 25 players to a side. Play began with both teams huddled over the ball kicking it until it popped free, a style similar to rugby. Players could push, pull, or carry teammates down the field. Ball carriers were permitted to crawl on the ground until held down.

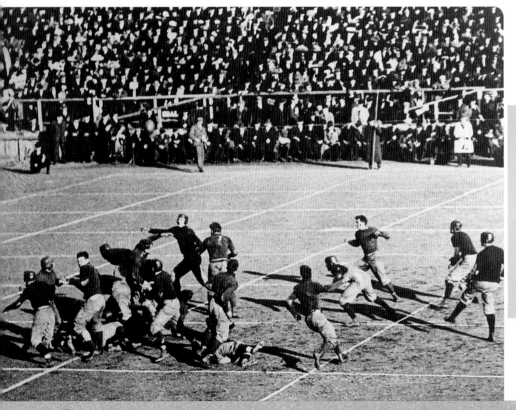

This photograph of a college football game was taken in the 1920s, when the games become popular. Notice that some of the players are not wearing helmets. Head protection was not mandatory in college football until 1939.

In 1873, representatives from Columbia, Rutgers, Princeton, and Yale universities met in New York City to establish the Intercollegiate Football Association (IFA). The schools agreed that 15 players, rather than 25, should be allowed on a side. Collegiate football became very popular, but by 1900, the brutality of the game had become a serious concern.

Because players did not wear helmets, severe concussions and even death from head injuries was a frequent occurrence.

Walter Camp

Walter Camp, who played for Yale University from 1877 until 1882, is generally considered the father of modern football. Camp, who also coached Yale from 1883 until 1910, transformed football from the rugby-type brawl to a sport with set plays and strategy. He set the length of the field at 100 yards and was responsible for limiting the players to eleven a side. He also started the "line of scrimmage" rule that begins play by giving the ball to one team. Initially the center began a play by kicking the ball back to a player behind the line of scrimmage. Camp later promoted rules to allow the center to "hike" or pass the ball between a person's legs to the quarterback.

The rise of the National Football League

The first professional football game is believed to have occurred in 1895 in the town of Latrobe, Pennsylvania, between a team representing that town and the team of Jeannette, Pennsylvania. In 1920, the American Professional Football Association was formed. In 1922, the league expanded to eighteen teams and moved into Wisconsin and New York, and was renamed the National Football League (NFL). By 1925, there were 22 NFL teams, but few pro teams had well-known stars.

Red Grange

Late that season, All-America halfback Harold (Red) Grange of the University of Illinois signed a contract to play with the Chicago Bears the day after his final collegiate game. The $3,000 contract was an enormous amount at a time when an entire team could be bought for $500. On Thanksgiving Day, a crowd of 36,000—the largest in pro football history—watched Grange play for the Bears against the Chicago Cardinals. Called the Galloping Ghost for his elusive moves, Grange's celebrity status persuaded a number of top college players to go professional. Because the popularity of football was based in colleges, the chance for fans to see stars from their favorite college teams led to wider interest in the NFL.

Football on television

The rise in fans for pro football took an enormous leap in the 1950s with the arrival of television in most American homes.

"Red" Grange was the most popular football player of the 1920s. At about 5-feet 10-inches tall and 175 pounds, Grange was small by modern football standards.

In 1951, a broadcast network (DuMont) paid $75,000 for the rights to broadcast the NFL Championship game coast-to-coast. In 1957, CBS became the first network to broadcast regular season NFL games to large cities across the country. In 1998 CBS paid $4 billion to televise the NFL's AFC games through 2005.

Television cameras positioned high over football stadiums give viewers a clear view of the football field. Televised football became enormously popular in the 1950s, and the game has become one of the most popular of all televised sports in the United States.

The greatest game ever played

The championship game between the Baltimore Colts and the New York Giants, played December 28, 1958, in Yankee Stadium is considered one of the greatest football games ever. A dozen eventual members of the Pro Football Hall of Fame were on the field that day.

The game ended with the score tied at seventeen. This led to the first sudden-death championship. Under the rules, the first team to score would win. The Giants got the ball first but were unable to move the ball and had to punt. The Colts, led by quarterback Johnny Unitas, moved the ball the length of the field and scored the winning touchdown.

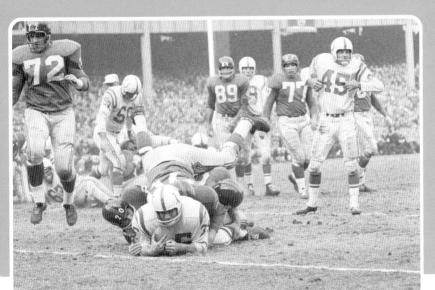

Football commissioner Bert Bell exclaimed, "This is the greatest day in the history of professional football!"

Equipment

Pro football is a dangerous game and it is vital that players wear the correct protective equipment. This can be separated into three categories: head protection, body protection, and leg protection.

Head protection

In football's early days, players let their hair grow all summer so that it would be long enough to protect their heads when the football season began in the fall. In the early years, most games were played without helmets. With the growth of college football's popularity in the 1920s, players wore leather helmets that were so light they could be folded in half and carried in a back pocket.

Nowadays players wear a hard plastic helmet with padding inside that protects the skull, face, and jaw from injury. All helmets are fitted with face masks to protect the front of a player's head and jaw. Players are also required to wear a mouth piece to protect the lips and teeth. It is form-fitted for the upper and lower teeth. The mouth piece is usually attached to the face mask so that it cannot be dropped.

Body protection

Shoulder pads protect the shoulder, chest, and upper back. Their size depends on a player's position. Pass receivers who need freedom of movement wear lighter pads, while ball carriers wear heavier pads to protect their upper bodies. Many linemen also wear arm and elbow pads to protect the forearms, elbows, and wrist.

Helmet fit fact

A football helmet should always
- cover the base of the skull
- have a gap of two finger widths above the eyebrows
- allow 1 to 1-1/2 inches between the nose and faceguard
- have chin strap centered under the point of the chin
- have ear holes aligned with ears
- have jaw pads tight against the side of the lower jaw
- remain motionless on the head

John Lujack, an All-American college football player, is shown wearing a standard football helmet from 1948. It consisted of a hard leather shell with thin padding protecting the head. Plastic helmets and face masks did not come into football until the 1950s.

Leg protection

All players wear athletic supporters and plastic cups for groin protection. In addition, they wear hip and tailbone pads. These lightweight foam pads are fitted in the football pants and worn to protect the bones of the pelvis and lower back. Thigh pads and knee pads are also required to protect the quadriceps muscles and knee joint.

All-Pro linebacker Ray Lewis of the Baltimore Ravens wears the standard pads of an NFL player, although the pads on his thighs are much smaller and lighter than those worn by linemen. Note that Lewis also wears padded gloves. These protect his fingers and help him hold onto the football if he tries to intercept a pass.

Helmet development

Helmets were not made mandatory in college football until 1939, and they were not required in pro football until 1943. By the early 1950s, scientists had developed hard plastic shells to replace the leather helmets. The facemask, which is today compulsory at all levels of football, did not appear until the mid-1950s. In 2002, Riddell introduced its first new model helmet in 25 years. The new model, called the Revolution (right), was developed to address the rise in concussions. Research showed that these head injuries were most often caused by blows to the side of the head and jaw, where padding and protection was weakest. The side of the new model drops down closer to the chin to provide better protection to the side of the head and the jaw.

Starting young

Trying out for an organized football team is a big step for a young player. For beginners, the best place to start is on town or local recreation programs. These programs emphasize proper methods of blocking and tackling so that players can avoid injury. At the beginning levels, winning is less important than developing basic skills and team unity.

Junior Player Development Program

In recent years, the National Football League has sponsored a Junior Player Development Program for young players aged twelve to fourteen. The six-week program teaches the basic moves of every position to every participant using methods developed by a group of professional, college, and high school coaches.

Every practice is divided into fifteen-minute segments. At the beginning of each segment, players work on their tackling and blocking technique or skills beginning just six inches apart to avoid jarring hits. By making sure they are in the right position before colliding, young players understand how to make contact without hurting themselves. Coaches point out that most injuries occur when players "duck" or pull back from contact.

Orphans in Iraq are taught the basics of football by U.S. soldiers based there in 2003. About 70 orphans took part altogether.

Flag football, in which players are "tackled" when flags are pulled from waist belts, is a popular form of recreational football for teenagers and college students. Informal leagues in towns and on campuses allow players to enjoy the basic games without the high-impact contact.

Footwork skills

Once the basic skill segment is complete, the basic footwork of a particular position is taught. All players may learn to back pedal, as pass defenders do in a game. In another session, they may learn the correct arm position to throw a pass. All practices end with a competition between teams that are selected by size and weight to avoid injury. The purpose of competition is not to win, but to have players correctly apply the skills learned that day.

The Junior Player coaches use practice to address young players about the connection between success on the field and success in life. Each week, a different life skill is introduced. These skills include responsibility, setting goals, sportsmanship, self-control, and teamwork.

Flag football

There are many sports fans who enjoy football but who want to avoid the collision of the full-contact sport. For these people, there are variations of football such as flag football.

Since 1996, the NFL has sponsored flag football leagues for boys and girls aged 6 to 14 in all 50 states. The 40-minute games have 5 players on a side. All players must wear a protective mouthpiece. To lessen the chance of injury, there are no kick-offs and no blocking is allowed. To make sure that there is plenty of action, all players are eligible to receive passes, including the quarterback. Players wear belts with flags attached by Velcro. Pulling a flag is the same thing as tackling a player with the ball. The ball is placed where the flag is dropped.

Weight training

There is no way around the fact that football is a game of strength. The best way to build strength, according to coaches, is by lifting weights. Weightlifting for young people was once thought to cause damage to the growth plates—areas of cartilage that had not yet turned to bone. Recent studies, however, have shown that weight training using free weights or machines is safe. In fact, research has shown that lifting weights increases the strength and firmness of bones, tendons, and ligaments, which in turn helps protect players from injury.

Developing fitness

The most important part of any weight training program, coaches agree, is supervision. Young players should never lift weights without a coach, trainer, or other adult nearby.

Another key is a warm-up. Warming up prepares an athlete for the challenge of a weight workout by increasing the heart rate. A light cardiovascular exercise such as jogging or jumping rope for three to five minutes is recommended. Fitness experts recommend that football players under age ten use body weight exercises only. A program for players this age would include push-ups, sit ups, vertical jumps, calf raises, and pull-ups.

After the age of ten, players can use exercise machines and light weights. Players beginning a weight training program should lift light weights until eight to twelve repetitions of an exercise can be performed.

To achieve gains in strength, workouts need to be at least 20 to 30 minutes two to three times per week.

One key to successful weight training is to train all muscles groups equally. Curls with dumbbells or barbells, for example, which build bicep muscles in the front of the upper arm should be followed by exercises that build the triceps in the back of the arm, such as standing presses.

Arm strength for football can be developed by weight training exercises such as the curl shown here. This exercise strengthens the forearm and upper arm, which in turn increases a player's ability to tackle and block an opponent.

Weight training exercises

Day 1: Arms
Biceps curls
Grip the bar wide, bend the knees, and keep good posture throughout the bicep workout.

Tricep pulldown (on cable machine)
Facing a cable machine, grip the handles shoulder width apart. With flexed knees, keep elbows in and pull down on the bar.

Day 2: Chest and upper back
Bench presses
Lying on bench with feet up, grip the bar about 8–10" outside the shoulders. Lower the weight down in a steady motion, so that it just touches the chest. Push barbell back up but do not lock elbows.

Shoulder shrugs
Grip the barbell approximately 6" wider than shoulders. Keep arms straight and head forward, while bringing shoulders up as high as possible.

Day 3: Legs
The leg press machine works all leg muscles except for the calves. Never lock the knees during the exercise. Bring the weight down so that the upper legs are parallel with the platform.

Calf raises
Hold a dumbbell in each hand on a stair step or box. Place the ball of the foot on the edge of the step. Stand on toes and hold for two seconds. Lower heels until parallel with the ground.

The dangers of steroids

In 2003, the football team from Buckeye High School in Buckeye, Arizona, lost its first three games. After that, things went from bad to worse. In late September, ten players were kicked off the team and suspended from school for using steroids.

Side effects

Many athletes do not understand that steroids are harmful. Steroids are drugs that were originally used to rebuild muscle tissue weakened by injury or illness. In the early 1960s, athletes discovered that taking abnormally large doses of steroids caused rapid gain in weight, strength, and speed. Steroids came into wide use among football players, weight lifters, and other athletes.

In the 1970s, doctors detected severe physical and mental side effects of steroid abuse. Among the physical side effects were heart disease, liver damage, hair loss, and severe skin eruptions. In addition, steroid use was linked to violent behavior known as "roid rage." Even more alarming for teenagers, studies showed that steroid use slowed the growth plates in adolescents' skeletal structure.

Lyle Alzado

In the 1970s and early 1980s, Lyle Alzado (left) was one of the most feared defensive linemen in pro football. Drafted by the Denver Broncos in 1971 as a 6-foot-3-inch, 255-pound defensive end, he grew into a 300-pound terror who was an All-Pro four times in his career before retirement in 1986.

In 1991, Alzado made a public appearance to acknowledge that he had terminal brain cancer. He said the cancer had resulted from his excessive use of steroids, which he began using in college in 1969. Alzado said that he had used steroids throughout his football career. He said that he had ignored doctors' warnings about the health effects of steroids and continued to use them after he retired from the game. Alzado died of brain cancer at age 42.

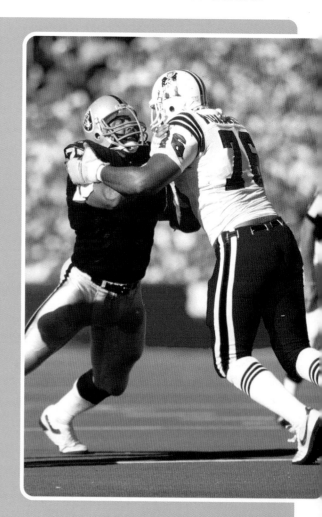

Laboratory tests for drugs can detect whether players are using steroids. A "positive" test can result in a suspension for a professional player and other punishments for college players.

the 1990s. Some young players, like those at Buckeye High School, learned the hard way that steroid use harmed not only them, but their team as well.

Steroids in schools

Despite these dangers, steroid use spread to high schools. A national drug survey in 2000 found that more than 479,000 students nationwide, or 2.9 percent, had used steroids by their senior year of high school. The survey reported that steroid use by teenagers had more than doubled in

Steroid penalty fact

In 1987, the NFL banned steroid use by players. A player who tests positive for using the drugs is suspended for four games for the first offense. Further use can result in being banned from the league.

Training and diet

Like all sports, training and diet are key ingredients of football success. Running two to three miles at least twice a week builds a player's basic fitness. After that, running should consist of short sprints and foot movement. No matter what position they play, football players must be agile enough to change direction quickly.

Agility drills

A popular agility drill for players who want to be running backs or receivers uses rows of truck tires. The tires are set close together in pairs, one for the left foot and one for the right. The players run down the row, lifting their knees up high as they go. This drill not only builds agility, it strengthens thigh and calf muscles.

An agility drill for linemen uses the "crab" movement—a somewhat awkward scrambling motion done on all fours. This position strengthens the hands, forearms, and shoulders. It also helps develop agility for line play when a player is knocked to the ground.

Players who want to play line positions can develop agility and leg strength by working against a blocking sled. This device has a smooth platform that supports two or more padded dummies. Players start forward from a lineman's stance, drive a shoulder into the dummy, and push the sled with their legs.

Food for energy

Nutrition experts say athletes should eat protein foods such as meat or beans for muscle and bone growth. Carbohydrates such as pasta, rice, and bread provide energy. Several servings per day of fruits and vegetables provide vitamins and minerals necessary to keep the body "machine" running smoothly. Bananas, for example, contain large amounts of the mineral potassium, which is lost when an athlete perspires. Lack of potassium can cause muscles to cramp, so it is a good idea for players to make bananas a regular part of the diet.

All-pro Larry Allen of the Dallas Cowboys is a 325-pound lineman with the speed and agility of a much smaller man. This combination makes him a devastating blocker as he leads running backs past defenders.

Athletes in training should drink up to sixteen ounces of liquid ten to fifteen minutes before exercise. During exercise they should drink four to six ounces of cold liquid every ten to fifteen minutes.

Jerry Rice

Over his career with the San Francisco 49ers and Oakland Raiders, wide receiver Jerry Rice has set fourteen NFL records, including career records for most receiving yardage and most receptions. In a sport in which the average career is less than five years, Rice has played nineteen seasons. In 2003, he became the only 40-year-old player to play in a Super Bowl. He attributes much of his success to his off-season fitness workout.

Rice's daily routine begins with a five-mile uphill run. As the season approaches he switches to sprints. That workout consists of 6 100-yard sprints, 6 of 80 yards, 6 of 60 yards, 6 40-yarders, 6 20s, and 16 10-yard sprints.

After his morning running, Rice lifts weights, alternating between his upper-body and lower-body. He then does three sets of 10 repetitions of 21 different exercises such as bench presses, shoulder pull-downs, calf raises, and thigh presses—a total of 630 repetitions for each workout.

Coaching

From the coaching point of view, football is unusual because a team is divided into separate offensive and defensive units. In addition, there are also special teams that perform only kicking plays. Professional teams may have as many as twenty coaches assisting the head coach. All coaches, however, look for the same qualities in players.

Effort

Most coaches would work with average players who give 100 percent effort than talented me-first players. Former Washington Redskins coach Marty Schottenheimer once cut his starting quarterback, Jeff George, because he felt that George was not trying hard enough to correct his mistakes during practice.

Enthusiasm

Coaches want players who love to practice as hard as they play. Players who are passionate about the sport help build team unity. During one summer practice, former Miami Dolphins coach Jimmy Johnson saw a relatively small unknown rookie making crushing tackles and encouraging his teammates. Johnson went over the player and said, "Son, you've made the team." The player was Zach Thomas, Miami's All-Pro linebacker.

Focus

Coaches look for players who pay close attention to every detail of the game. They organize each day's practice to the minute. They expect players to know their assignment— and every other player's assignment— for every play. When Andy Reid applied for the job as head coach of the Philadelphia Eagles in 1998, he

Coach Marty Schottenheimer became a professional coach after as successful career as player. He expects his players to play as hard as he once did; those who do not give maximum effort are cut from the team.

came to the interview carrying two thick notebooks. One notebook was filled with offensive plays and notes on each Eagle player. The other was a defensive notebook on Eagle defensive players. Reid had never coached the players, but had already made detailed notes about the teams. He was hired.

Vince Lombardi

In 1958, Vince Lombardi became the head coach for the Green Bay Packers, a team that had won only one game that season. He told his players that with obedience, dedication, and effort they could become champions. Three years later, the Packers won the NFL championship. Under Lombardi, the Packers won five NFL championships and the first two Super Bowls. He became famous for his observations about football and its connection to life. Among his most well known quotes are:

"The quality of a person's life is in direct proportion to their commitment to excellence, regardless of their chosen field of endeavor."

"The difference between a successful person and others is not a lack of strength, nor a lack of knowledge, but rather in a lack of will."

"It's not whether you get knocked down, it's whether you get up."

Sportsmanship

Coaches do not want trash talkers or players who celebrate after every play.

In 2000, then San Francisco 49ers coach Steve Mariucci watched his All-Pro wide receiver Terrell Owens, now of the Philadelphia Eagles, run from the end zone to the center of the field after a score and spike the ball. His taunting provoked the Cowboys and a fight ensued. Even though Owens was his best player, Mariucci suspended him for the next two games.

Coach John Gruden led the Tampa Bay Buccaneers to the Super Bowl championship in 2003. He is legendary for his hard work, often working eighteen hours a day, seven days a week, during the six-month professional season.

Quarterbacks

NFL quarterbacks such as Peyton Manning or Brett Favre can easily throw a football 50 yards or more in a spiral with pinpoint accuracy. What they make look easy, however, is the result of practice and constant repetition. Passing a football can be broken down into four separate steps.

The grip

The fingers should be spread lightly across the laces, but the ball should not touch the palm of the hand. The strongest points of the grip should be from the thumb, middle, and ring fingers. The thumb and forefinger should form a "U" at the tail of the ball.

and take a small step forward with the front foot. The throwing shoulder is moved forward. The upper arm should remain parallel to the ground as the ball comes forward, and the lower arm should extend from the elbow.

Stance and delivery

The player should stand sideways with the ball at shoulder height and the non-throwing hip facing the target. The ball is cocked behind the ear. The player must push off the back foot

Brett Favre of the Green Bay Packers displays a perfect passing stance before releasing the ball. Note how Favre is stepping forward with opposite leg to gain distance on his pass.

Release

The player should rotate the forearm outward, and snap the wrist. The ball is allowed to spin out of the hand from the little finger to the index finger.

Follow through

The throwing arm should be completely extended as the ball is released. The arm must follow through until the palm faces the ground. The player should step forward with the back leg until the feet are nearly parallel. The knees should always be kept bent. The wrist-snap that spins or spirals the ball can be difficult to learn. Beginners may want to allow the ball to rotate from the flat of the hand to the fingertips.

The class of 1983

Each year, NFL teams draft the most promising college football players. The most sought-after college players are usually quarterbacks, the players who direct a team's offense.

In 1983, 6 of the first 28 players chosen were quarterbacks—a draft record. All six quarterbacks had successful careers, and three of them are or will soon become members of the Pro Football Hall of Fame. They are John Elway of the Denver Broncos, Jim Kelly *(right)* of the Buffalo Bills, and Dan Marino of the Miami Dolphins. Elway, Kelly, and Marino all lead their teams to the Super Bowl. Marino lost in his only appearance but holds several all-time NFL passing records, including most yards gained. Kelly took the Bills to four straight Super Bowls but never won the game. Elway lost two Super Bowls and won two. He holds an NFL record of 41, 4th-quarter game-saving drives. Kelly was voted into the Hall of Fame in 2003. Elway was nominated in 2004. Marino will be in 2005.

Running backs

A modern running back must carry the ball between 20 and 30 times a game and block defensive players rushing the quarterback. He must also catch passes. Multi-talented backs such as Marshall Faulk of the St. Louis Rams have the speed to outrun defenders, good hands to catch passes, and blocking skills to pick up defensive players. Although the position of running back may have changed, many of football's basic running plays have remained unchanged.

Off-tackle

One of the oldest running plays begins with the running back (RB right) taking the handoff and running toward the end of the line where the tight end—an extra blocker—lines up. The runner follows his backfield partner, the fullback (FB), around the "wall" created by the tackle and tight end. This play works best with big running backs such as 230-pound Stephen Davis of the Carolina Panthers.

Draw

This is a run that looks like a pass play at first. The offensive linemen step back as they would if they were planning to pass-protect. The

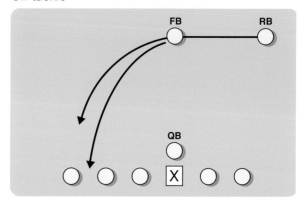

Off-tackle

quarterback drops back as he would to pass but instead hands the ball to the runner. After the runner receives the ball, he accelerates past defenders who rush past him thinking the play is a pass. Cat-quick running backs such as Warrick Dunn of the Atlanta Falcons excel at draw plays.

Running back Ricky Williams of the Miami Dolphins shows perfect form on an off-tackle run. Note how the ball is tucked under arm opposite the players blocking. This helps protect the ball from being knocked loose.

Pitch

In this play, the quarterback fakes a handoff to the first back, who heads directly into the line of scrimmage to draw defenders toward him. The quarterback then pitches the ball laterally to the other runner (RB below), who races around the end. Fast backs who cut quickly such as Clinton Portis of the Washington Redskins can beat defenders around the end of the line on a pitch.

Pitch

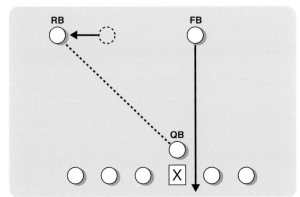

Single game rushing record

At 5 feet, 11 inches and 235 pounds, running back Jamal Lewis of the Baltimore Ravens has the power to run over tacklers. He also has the speed of an Olympic sprinter to outrun defenders. On September 14, 2003, Lewis used both power and speed to set a new record for yards gained in a single game. He ran for 295 yards as the Ravens defeated the Cleveland Browns 33-13.

Lewis's total broke the record set in 2000 by Corey Dillon of the Cincinnati Bengals who ran for 278 yards. Before that mark, Hall of Fame runner, the late Walter Payton of the Chicago Bears, had set the record of 275 yards in 1977.

Receivers

In football's early days, pass receivers were called ends because their position was next to the tackle at the end of the line. Modern football has changed the role of pass-catching players. The traditional end is now called the tight end. He is a large receiver who plays close to the tackle, blocks, and runs short pass patterns in the middle of the field. In addition, most teams also use a split end, who is "split" several yards from the tackle. The best receiver on the team is usually called the wide receiver—these are the gifted athletes who haul in the long bomb passes such as Randy Moss of the Minnesota Vikings.

Running patterns

The main responsibility of all receivers is to get open for a pass by running patterns designed to fake the defender into turning in the wrong direction. Most patterns begin with a receiver attempting to break free of the man guarding him at the line of scrimmage. In some cases, the pattern is simply a streak down the field at full speed (see diagram).

Randy Moss of the Minnesota Vikings excels at faking the streak, then cutting diagonally across the field for a post route. His height— 6 feet 4 inches—and his great leaping ability make him an inviting target for quarterbacks.

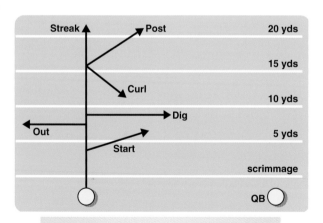

Most pass patterns are based off the streak. By faking a straight ahead route downfield, a receiver can fool a defender and cut in either direction to get open.

An out

A 90-degree cut toward the sideline. It is a mid- to short-range pattern for a quick pass. Receivers who can make precise split-second cuts such as Laveranues Coles of the Washington Redskins are hard to defend on an out pattern, which is run to the side of the field where the ball is closest the sideline.

A curl

A receiver sprints downfield then stops suddenly and turns or curls toward the quarterback. Big tight ends such as Jeremy Shockey of the New York Giants who catch the ball over shorter defenders make the curl an effective mid-range pass play.

A post

A receiver sprints straight ahead then cuts suddenly at a 45 degree angle and runs toward the goal post. Tall, fast receivers such as Terrell Owens of the Philadelphia Eagles run this pattern for long gains and touchdowns.

Marvin Harrison

In six years in the NFL, wide receiver Marvin Harrison of the Indianapolis Colts has teamed with quarterback Peyton Manning to make one of the most effective combinations in NFL history. In 80 games, Manning has completed 549 passes to Harrison for 7,351 yards and 62 touchdowns. In 2002, Harrison of the Indianapolis Colts set the NFL record for most passes caught in a season—143.

Harrison's quick footwork allows him to elude a defender's grasp at the line of scrimmage. He also runs precise patterns—if a pattern is a twenty yard curl, he runs exactly twenty yards. This precision allows Manning to simply throw to point on the field, knowing that Harrison will be there when the ball arrives. Harrison also shares the trait of all great receivers: he is always open for a pass.

Pass catching tip

Catch the ball with hands in front of body, touching the thumbs and index fingers to form a diamond shape.

Offensive line

A good lineman must have a combination of size, speed, strength, and, intelligence. What is generally considered the offensive line consists of five players: the center, two guards, and two tackles.

Lineup

The center is in the middle of the line and snaps the ball to the quarterback. He also calls out blocking assignments to his linemates before a play begins.

Two guards line up on either side of the center. These are the fastest linemen and lead runners on running plays around the outside of the line of scrimmage.

Beside the guards are the two tackles. They are usually the largest of the linemen and are assigned to wall off the quarterback from pass rushers.

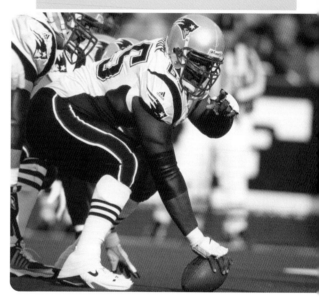

Center Damien Woody, who signed with Detroit prior to the 2004 season, points out blocking assignments for his former team, the New England Patriots. Centers usually call out the blocking assignments to other linemen before the ball is snapped.

Guard Larry Allen who moves extremely fast for a large man, leads a running play around the outside of the defensive line.

Average size fact

The average size of a lineman has increased over the years:

1930s: 6', 230 lbs

1950s: 6' 2", 240 lbs

1970s: 6' 3", 260 lbs

1990s: 6' 4", 300 lbs

Successful tactics

Whatever position a lineman plays, there are two key elements to success.

- Proper stance: A lineman's feet should be a little more than shoulder width apart with the knees bent over the toes. The back should be straight and the body bent at the hips with the right hand (for right-handed players) placed on the ground. Chris Samuels, left tackle of the Washington Redskins, weighs more than 320 pounds, but his big body is well balanced, so he can move in any direction at the snap of the ball.

- Quick start. A lineman should explode into his opponent at the snap of the ball and stay low. He should punch up with the palms of his hands, to the numbers of the defender in a lifting motion. Larry Allen, the All-Pro guard of the Dallas Cowboys, weighs 340 pounds, but he is so quick that he can block defenders before they react, which opens holes for runners. Also, the lineman should always try to get lower than a charging defensive player in pass blocking. The lower player has better leverage.

Orlando Pace

In the annual NFL draft, only one offensive lineman has been a number one choice since 1968—Orlando Pace, the number one choice of the St. Louis Rams in 1997. At 6-feet 7-inches and 320 pounds, Pace, a left tackle, was so dominant in college that a new sports statistic was invented for him. It was called the pancake, and it signified a play in which Pace knocked his opponent backward off his feet during a running play.

By 1999, Pace was an All-Pro, and the St. Louis offense gained the most passing yards in NFL history. Although he pass-blocked hundreds of times, Pace was not called for a single holding penalty—illegally using his hands to stop a pass rusher—during the entire season while he protected quarterback Kurt Warner. Warner was named the NFL's Most Valuable Player.

In 2000, Pace again blocked for a Most Valuable Player—running back Marshall Faulk, who scored a record 26 touchdowns.

Defensive line

The primary purpose of the defensive line is to stop ball carriers and sack quarterbacks. For example the nose tackle lines up directly across from the center. He engages blockers to free other defenders to make tackles. Pro nose tackles usually weigh 300 pounds or more.

Obstructing blockers

Defensive tackles line up inside the defensive ends, usually opposite the offensive guards. Like the nose tackle, they obstruct blockers, but they make more tackles and rush the passer. Cat-quick at 6 feet and 305 pounds, defensive tackle Warren Sapp of the Oakland Raiders is almost impossible to block.

Defensive ends line up over the offensive tackles or on those players' outside shoulders. They are responsible for preventing end runs and tackling the quarterback before

he passes. These players are usually the lightest and the fastest of the defensive linemen. At 6 feet 7 inches and 260 pounds, Jason Taylor of the Miami Dolphins is fast enough to run around big tackles and tall enough to knock down passes.

A good defensive lineman must be strong enough to shove an offensive lineman out of the way. He must also be durable because he is blocked on every play. Smart defensive linemen also "read" the stances of the offensive linemen to gain an advantage. For

Warren Sapp (in red) sacks Oakland Raiders' quarterback Rich Gannon in the NFL Superbowl XXXVII in 2003. In 2004, Sapp left Tampa Bay and signed with Oakland Raiders.

example, if an offensive lineman leans his weight on his hand, a defender knows he will probably move forward and block for a run. If the offensive lineman has his weight on his heels and head raised, he will likely be staying in place for pass protection.

Defensive line nicknames fact

Defensive lines for winning teams often have nicknames. Some of the best defensive lines were:

Fearsome Foursome—Los Angeles Rams, 1960s

Purple People Eaters—Minnesota Vikings, 1970s

Orange Crush—Denver Broncos, 1970s

Steel Curtain—Pittsburgh Steelers, 1970s

New York Sack Exchange—New York Jets, 1980s

Michael Strahan's sack record

In the 2001–2002 season, All-Pro defensive end Michael Strahan of the New York Giants terrorized opposing quarterbacks. By the last game of the season, he had 21 1/2 sacks—a half-sack is awarded when two defenders tackle the quarterback. The record of 22 sacks had been set in 1984.

Strahan needed just one sack in a game against the Green Bay Packers to break the record, but the Green Bay offensive line kept him away from quarterback Brett Favre. Late in the game, the ball was snapped and Favre faked a pass, ran towards Strahan, and slid at his feet. Strahan touched Favre to make certain he was down. Technically, because Favre faked a pass and was touched down by Strahan, it counted as a sack. Strahan broke the record, but many fans considered the final sack questionable.

Linebackers

Linebacker are defensive players positioned in the back of the defensive line. Inside or middle linebackers have responsibility for stopping ball carriers and pass receivers in the middle of the field. Outside linebackers are responsible for plays around the end.

Mobile, agile, and hostile

Pro coach "Bum" Phillips of the Houston Oilers in the 1970s once said that linebackers must be "mobile, agile, and hostile." Because linebackers must cover large areas of the field, they must be fast. Because they take on blockers, they need to be agile. Because their play sets the tone for the defense, linebackers also have to be ferocious tacklers. Hall of Famer Lawrence Taylor changed entire games when he crunched opposing quarterbacks or receivers with vicious tackles.

Linebackers are the quarterbacks of the defense. They must know the position, run responsibility, and pass responsibility for every player in every defense formation. Once the defense lines up across from the offense, linebackers must recheck every player's positioning. If a teammate lines up incorrectly, it is the linebacker's job to move him into position before the ball is snapped. Ray Lewis, middle linebacker of the Baltimore Ravens, calls position adjustments right until the ball is snapped.

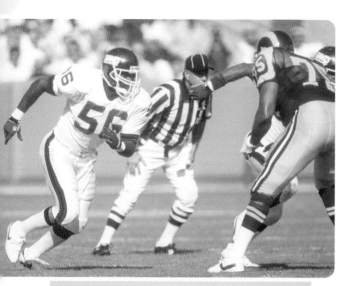

Lawrence Taylor of the New York Giants was one of the most feared pass-rushing linebackers in pro football history. Faster than most running backs, the 240-pound Taylor was too fast for linemen to block, and his devastating hits on quarterbacks made him a favorite of Giants' fans.

Tackling tips

The basic tackle consists of several steps

1. Approach the ball carrier with feet shoulder width apart

2. Keep knees bent.

3. Lean upper body slightly forward.

4. Head up! Avoid any contact to the top of the head. Lowering the head prior to contact, even slightly, can result in serious injury.

5. Wrap the ball carrier with the arms and shoulders. Imagine lifting the shoulder pads off the opponent.

Most linebackers spend hours off the field preparing for an opponent. They study films of an opponent's games to learn their offense's strengths and weaknesses. The best linebackers can recognize what play is coming when they see a specific offensive formation.

Linebacker Ray Lewis of the Baltimore Ravens uses his blazing speed to "sack" quarterback Steve McNair (9) of the Tennessee Titans before he can pass the ball.

The violent world of Sam Huff

After the exciting overtime championship game of 1958, TV executives decided to build pro football's appeal by giving viewers a close look—and listen—to the hitting on the field. In 1959, Sam Huff, middle linebacker of the New York Giants was filmed during the Giants' training camp and exhibition games. The revolutionary idea of taping microphones in Huff's shoulder pads allowed viewers to hear every collision.

In early 1960, the documentary "The Violent World of Sam Huff" was broadcast on CBS. The documentary did a great deal to create a television audience for pro football. Huff became on overnight celebrity at age 24. His fame was increased by the success of the Giants, who won one championship and appeared in six title games in his eight seasons (1956–1963). He was later traded to the Washington Redskins and retired in 1969.

Defensive backs

In the defensive backfield the cornerbacks—left and right—cover the wide receiver and split end. They are also responsible for stopping running plays toward their side of the field. Charles Woodson of the Oakland Raiders excels at covering receivers, because of his quick feet and ability to anticipate a receiver's route.

Safeties

Behind the cornerbacks are two safeties. The strong safety lines up opposite the tight end. The strong safety is usually the biggest defensive back and makes many tackles on running plays. At 6 feet and 230 pounds, strong safety Roy Williams of the Dallas Cowboys is almost as big as linebacker, yet he has sprinter's speed and can cover an opposing team's biggest receiver.

The free safety is the fastest defensive back and must make sure that no receiver gets behind him. Brian Dawkins of the Philadelphia Eagles weighs just 200 pounds, but his timing and explosive speed enable him to crush receivers after a catch.

Safety Brian Dawkins heads up field after intercepting a pass. Note that Dawkins is holding the ball away from his body. This is dangerous, because an opponent can knock the ball loose with a hard hit.

Defensive backs must be able to run backward as fast as the fastest receiver runs forward. They must also be able to watch the quarterback and the receiver and knock down a pass or intercept it without touching the receiver while the ball is in the air. In addition, defensive backs must break up running plays while fighting off blockers who outweigh them by more than 100 pounds.

In most cases, defensive backs play two types of pass defense—man-to-man and zone. In man-to-man, a defensive back stays with his assigned receiver no matter where he runs. The defensive back does everything possible to get the receiver's mind off catching the football. Within five yards of the line of scrimmage, they can use their hands to knock a receiver off stride.

You can't do that

Defensive backs must follow strict rules. Pass defense penalties harm a team at critical times:

Illegal contact: After a receiver is five yards beyond the line of scrimmage, the defensive player cannot grab, hold, or shove the receiver, thus knocking him off his intended pass route. The penalty is an automatic first down.

Pass interference. A defensive player may not restrict a receiver's opportunity to gain position or to catch the ball. This penalty is an automatic first down, and the ball is placed at the spot of the foul. If interference occurs in the end zone, the offense gets a first down on the one-yard line.

In the zone defense, the defensive backs stand between five and ten yards off the line of scrimmage. This means that they cannot touch or "chuck" a receiver. Instead, they cover any player who comes into their assigned area of the field. This defense requires good communication between the cornerbacks and the safeties when a receiver leaves one player's zone and runs to another.

Pass defense tips

Pass defenders should watch the quarterback while they cover a receiver. Never lose track of the ball.

Dexter Jackson (left) of the Tampa Bay Buccaneers makes an interception in Super Bowl XXXVII against the Oakland Raiders. The Buccaneers defensive backs made five interceptions in the game, which Tampa Bay won 48–21.

The kicking game

While many football fans are excited by powerful running backs, fleet wide receivers, and tough-hitting defenders, it is often the team's smallest players who make the biggest difference in a game. These are the kickers—who kick from a tee or held ball—and the punters—who kick the ball by dropping it on their foot.

Kickers

In football's early days, kickers approached the ball straight-on and kicked with a square-toe shoe. Today, most kickers use a soccer-style kick. With this method, the kicker approaches the ball from an angle and strikes it with the shoe-laced portion of the foot.

Kickers aim for a point on the opposite side of the ball from the laces about one-third of the way from the bottom. Contact above this point will create a low kick, which is likely to be blocked. If contact is made below the ideal point, the ball will rotate too fast, creating a high arc that will shorten the distance of the ball.

Whether kicking for points or kicking off after a score, the best kickers keep their head down and eyes on the ball. They do not raise their eyes until the ball has left the foot. During the final part of the kick, a follow-through should bring the body facing straight toward the goal post.

Kicker Jason Hanson of the Detroit Lions is considered one the most accurate kickers in the NFL. Note the height of his kicking leg as he follows through on a field goal attempt.

Why kicking matters

In September 2003, the New York Giants made a strong comeback against the Dallas Cowboys. Losing for most of the game, the Giants went ahead 32 to 29 when Matt Bryant kicked a 30-yard field goal with 11 seconds left in the game. All the Giants had to do was kick off to the Cowboys and hold them for 11 seconds.

Unfortunately for the Giants, Bryant's kickoff bounced out of bounds at the one-yard line. The penalty for kicking out of bounds gave the ball to the Cowboys at their own 40-yard line. A Dallas pass of 25 yards put the Cowboys on the New York 34. Cowboy kicker Billy Cundiff tied the game as time ran out.

In sudden-death overtime, the Cowboys moved the ball into Giant territory. Cundiff tied the NFL record with his 7th field goal, which gave the Cowboys a 35-32 victory.

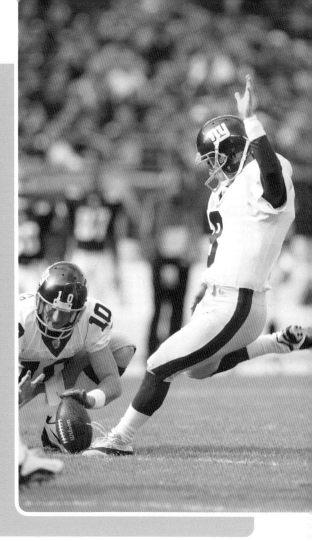

Punters

Punters differ from place kickers because they drop the ball after receiving a long snap from the center. Kickers take two steps— a right footed kicker steps right, then left, then kicks. They kick straight up through the ball with a forward body lean follow-through.

The man considered the greatest punter in football history, Ray Guy of the Oakland Raiders, extended his foot above his head in a perfectly straight line up from his right hip.

Successful punters work for years to develop the flexibility of the kicking leg to allow them to follow through on the ball.

Injuries

According to studies, fewer than two percent of football injuries result in hospital stays. Most football injuries are either strains, sprains, or bruises.

Strains

When muscles are stretched too far, too suddenly, they can be strained or pulled. Tight, thick muscles—such as those in the leg—are often more susceptible to injury, so athletes should stretch and warm up thoroughly before any exercise.

Sprains

Sprains are injuries to ligaments, the tissue that connects bone to bone within the joints of the knees, ankles, and shoulders. In mild, first-degree sprains, some fibers of a ligament are torn, there is swelling but no loss of movement. In second-degree sprains, the ligament is torn and there is more swelling and some loss of movement. Severe, third-degree sprains tear the ligament from one of its attachments or pull it apart, causing complete loss of movement.

The most common serious knee injury occurs when the anterior cruciate ligament (ACL) is torn. The ACL crosses the front of the knee and prevents the bones that form the joint from sliding forwards and back. An ACL tear may require surgery to repair.

Bruises

Bruised muscles are caused by impacts that break blood vessels in the muscle tissue. Large muscles in the legs or upper arms can bleed quite heavily. Ice is used to control swelling, relieve pain, and reduce recovery time. Although bruised muscles generally are not serious, if discomfort lasts more than a week, a doctor should be consulted.

Trainers and sports medicine specialists say that the worst thing a football player can do with an injury is "walk it off" or "work through it." To do so, they say, can allow minor injuries to become recurring problems and harm an athlete's health and performance.

A trainer helps an injured lineman off the field. Although most injuries are bumps and bruises, a trainer is important because he or she can diagnose a more severe injury.

Concussion fact

Football players are at high risk of having concussions over the course of their career. A concussion occurs when the brain, which is suspended in fluid, hits the inside of the skull after the head has been struck. Symptoms of concussion depend on how severely the brain has been injured. They range from headaches, dizziness, nausea, vomiting, confusion, blurred vision, and ringing in the ears, to double vision and sometimes loss of consciousness.

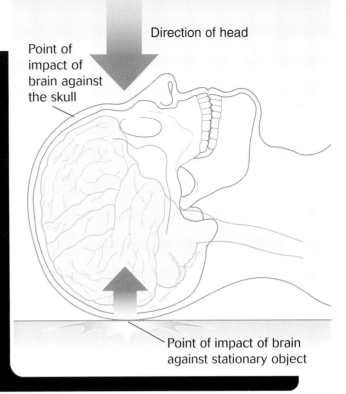

Direction of head

Point of impact of brain against the skull

Point of impact of brain against stationary object

Courageous comeback

In October 2000, Neil Parry was a freshman football player for San Jose State University in San Jose, California. On the opening kickoff against the University of

Texas at El Paso, Parry suffered a severely broken right leg. Infections developed while he was in the hospital that resulted in the leg being amputated below the knee.

In 2003, after 25 operations and thousands of hours spent in physical therapy, Parry was ready to play again. On September 13, wearing number 32, he took the field for warm-ups. Parry then joined two teammates as team captains for the pregame coin toss. In doing so, he became the first player ever to suit up for college football game with a prosthetic, or artificial, limb.

Late in the game, Parry came onto the field as part of the punt return team. It was his first action since the game almost three years earlier. The crowd chanted "Parry! Parry!" as he lined up. The ball was kicked to a San Jose return man, and Parry hit two players. That was his only game action, but the crowd gave him a standing ovation as he left the field.

Game day

A typical game day for a football team begins with a pregame meal about three to four hours before game time. In most cases, the meals include pasta or other carbohydrate-heavy food such as potatoes. Foods such as peanut butter, lean meat, low-fat cheese, or whole grain cereal with low-fat milk are common. Fats are avoided because they can upset the stomach during exercise.

Pregame

After the meal, the team breaks into various groups for position meetings with coaches. There they discuss key plays or players on the other team.

After position meetings, the long process of getting into uniform begins. All players must have their ankles taped. Players who are playing with injuries may require special taping and padding.

The team then goes onto the field where they stretch their muscles. Some players—especially linemen—may then pair off for light contact drills. Quarterbacks and receivers play catch or run basic patterns. Kickers and punters kick from increasing distances and note the wind direction and the footing on the field.

After players have broken into a light sweat, they return to the locker room where they make any adjustments to equipment. If the field is muddy or frozen, for example, players may change shoes. The head coach then addresses the entire team with encouragement, a motivational speech, or perhaps strategy.

Game day atmosphere for a college game is heightened by the music of the marching bands. The University of Michigan band plays to crowds of more than 100,000 people.

The game begins

With less than a half-hour until kickoff, players go to their team benches. Team captains walk to the middle of the field where they meet officials and the opposing captains. Officials flip a coin, and the team that wins makes the choice of whether to kick off or receive the football. The losing team then selects which end of the field they want to start the game. By this time, fans are excited and starting line-ups are announced. The national anthem is performed, and the game begins.

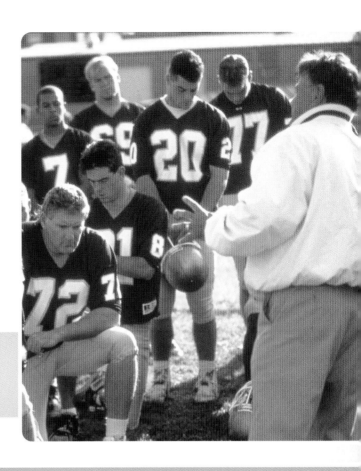

Coaches always go over final instructions with players in the pregame warmups. The players in this photo have not put on their shoulder pads yet, so there is about an hour to kickoff.

Getting stoked

Part of preparing for a football game is "getting stoked" to play. That means building up the aggression and energy required to endure sixty minutes of violent collisions and maintaining that aggression for every play. Because football is a team game, players often feed off the energy of their teammates rather than the coach. In the huddle of the offensive team (see photo), it is the job of the quarterback not only to call the plays, but to implore his teammates to give 100 percent effort.

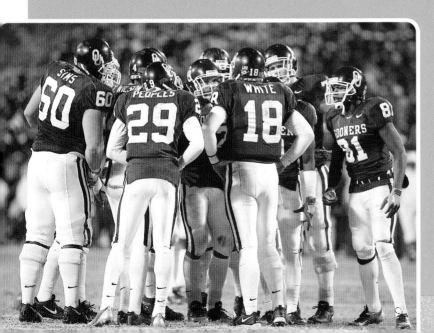

In the defensive huddle, it is generally the middle linebacker who is the leader. He challenges his teammates to stop opponents in key situations.

In many cases, players on opposing teams are physically equal—big, fast, and strong. The team that wins may be the team with a psychological edge.

What it takes to make a champion

In 2003 the minimum salary for a first-year pro football player was $225,000. Although that figure is less than the minimum first-year salaries in professional basketball and baseball, it is still a lot of money to many athletes who dream of playing pro football.

Grocer to pro

For quarterback Kurt Warner, the minimum salary was a fortune. After graduating from college in 1994, Warner tried out for the Green Bay Packers. He was cut in training camp, and it appeared that his chance at pro football was gone. In 1995 and 1996, Warner had to take a job bagging groceries in a supermarket to support his family.

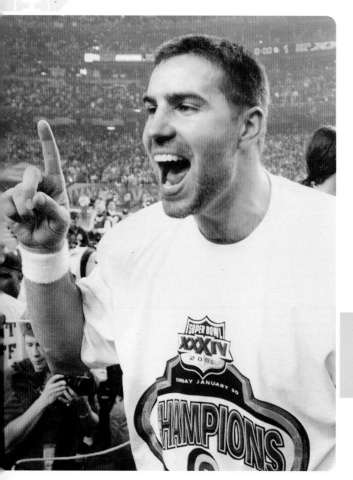

Nevertheless, Warner refused to quit on his dream of playing pro football. He worked out on his own and called various NFL teams for a tryout. In 1998, Warner played professional football in Europe, hoping to show his abilities to NFL teams. The St. Louis Rams signed him to a contract.

By 1999, Warner was a backup player, earning $250,000—slightly more than the minimum rate. In a preseason game, the Rams' starting quarterback injured his knee and was lost for the season. Suddenly, Warner became a starting quarterback in the NFL.

In the first four games, Warner shocked pro football by throwing more touchdown passes—fourteen—than any player in NFL history over a four-game period. By the end of the season, Warner was named the league's Most Valuable Player.

Quarterback Kurt Warner celebrates after leading his team—the St. Louis Rams—to a last-minute victory against the Tennessee Titans in Super Bowl XXXIV.

In the Super Bowl XXXV, Warner passed for a Super Bowl record 424 yards, including a game-winning 73-yard touchdown pass with less than 2 minutes to play, to help the Rams defeat the Tennessee Titans. In a few short years, he had gone from supermarket bagger to Super Bowl champion.

Joe Namath's guarantee

In the first two Super Bowls, which were played between the American Football League (AFL) and the NFL before they merged, the NFL's Green Bay Packers beat the Oakland Raiders 33-14 and the Kansas City Chiefs, 35-10. The NFL was widely considered the dominant league. In 1969, the mighty Baltimore Colts of the NFL were favored to win by eighteen points over the AFL team, the New York Jets.

Joe Namath, however, did not believe his team would lose. The New York Jets' quarterback was the most outspoken player in football. Several days before Super Bowl III, Namath "guaranteed" that the Jets would win. Sports fans were shocked. In those days, players did not make such claims. It was one of the boldest predictions ever made in pro football history. During the game, however, Namath backed up his words leading the Jets to an unexpected victory. The Jets not only won 16-7, Namath was the MVP, completing 17 of 28 passes for 206 yards. While many players in other sports have "guaranteed" victory in important games, few backed it up like Namath. His confidence inspired his teammates, and they followed his leadership.

Some major NFL records

Among the most prestigious NFL records are those for the most yards gained by running backs, and various passing records held by quarterbacks.

Individual and Team Records/Facts	
Record	**Holder/s**
Longest field goal	Tom Dempsey, New Orleans Saints (1970)
	Jason Elam, Denver Broncos (1998)
Most touchdowns in a career	Jerry Rice, 192
Only team to go undefeated for an entire season	Miami Dolphins, 14-0 in 1972
First team to decorate their helmets	Los Angeles Rams, 1948
Team never to have a player return a kickoff for a touchdown	Tampa Bay Buccaneers, since their first season in 1975
Oldest nickname in pro football	The Packers, they were founded in 1919 as a team sponsored by the Green Bay (Wisc) Indian Packers, a meat-packing company.

Super Bowl Champions			
Year	**Team**	**Year**	**Team**
1967	Green Bay Packers (NFL)	1986	Chicago Bears
1968	Green Bay Packers (NFL)	1987	New York Giants
1969	New York Jets (AFL)	1988	Washington Redskins
1970	Kansas City Chiefs (AFL)	1989	San Francisco 49ers
1971	Baltimore Colts	1990	San Francisco 49ers
1972	Dallas Cowboys	1991	New York Giants
1973	Miami Dolphins	1992	Washington Redskins
1974	Miami Dolphins	1993	Dallas Cowboys
1975	Pittsburgh Steelers	1994	Dallas Cowboys
1976	Pittsburgh Steelers	1995	San Francisco 49ers
1977	Oakland Raiders	1996	Dallas Cowboys
1978	Dallas Cowboys	1997	Green Bay Packers
1979	Pittsburgh Steelers	1998	Denver Broncos
1980	Pittsburgh Steelers	1999	Denver Broncos
1981	Oakland Raiders	2000	St. Louis Rams
1982	San Francisco 49ers	2001	Baltimore Ravens
1983	Washington Redskins	2002	New England Patriots
1984	Los Angeles Raiders	2003	Tampa Bay Buccaneers
1985	San Francisco 49ers	2004	New England Patriots

NFL All-time Leading Rushers, Most Yards Gained, Career

Yards	Player	Team (Years)
17,162	Emmitt Smith	Dallas (1990–2002) Arizona (2003–
16,726	Walter Payton	Chicago (1975–1987)
15,269	Barry Sanders	Detroit (1989–1998)
13,259	Eric Dickerson	L.A. Rams (1983–1987), Indianapolis (1987–1991),
		L.A. Raiders (1992), Atlanta (1993)
12,739	Tony Dorsett	Dallas (1977–1987), Denver (1988)
12,312	Jim Brown	Cleveland (1957–1965)
12,243	Marcus Allen	L.A. Raiders (1982–1992), Kansas City (1993–1997)
12,120	Franco Harris	Pittsburgh (1972–1983), Seattle (1984)
12,074	Thurman Thomas	Buffalo (1988–1999), Miami (2000)
11,542	Jerome Bettis	L.A. Rams (1993–1994)
		St. Louis Rams (1995) Pittsburgh (1996–

Leading Lifetime Passers, Minimum 1,500 attempts (At the Start of 2003 Season)

Rank	Player	Yrs	Att	Comp	Yds	TD	INT	Rating
1 (-)	Kurt Warner	5	1,623	1,083	14,082	10	164	98.2
2 (1)	Steve Young	15	4,149	2,667	33,124	232	107	96.8
3 (2)	Joe Montana*	15	5,391	3,409	40,551	273	139	92.3
4 (-)	Jeff Garcia	4	1,968	1,224	13,704	95	43	89.9
5 (3)	Brett Favre	12	5,993	3,652	42,285	314	188	86.7
6 (4)	Otto Graham*	10	2,626	1,464	23,584	174	135	86.6
7 (5)	Dan Marino	17	8,358	4,967	61,361	420	252	86.4
8 (6)	Peyton Manning	5	2,817	1,749	20,618	138	100	85.9
9 (11)	Rich Gannon	14	3,913	2,367	26,945	171	98	85.3
10 (7)	Mark Brunell	9	3,561	2,142	25,309	142	86	85.1
11 (10)	Brad Johnson	11	2,831	1,747	19,428	114	74	84.6

* Pro Football Hall of Fame Member

Leading Lifetime Receivers (At the Start of 2003 Season)

Rank	Player	Yrs	No.	Yds	Avg	TD
1 (1)	Jerry Rice	18	1,456	21,597	14.8	192
2 (2)	Cris Carter	16	1,101	13,899	12.6	130
3 (5)	Tim Brown	15	1,018	14,167	13.9	97
4 (3)	Andre Reed	16	951	13,198	13.9	87
5 (4)	Art Monk	16	940	12,721	13.5	68
6 (6)	Irving Fryar	17	851	12,785	15.0	84
7 (7)	Steve Largent*	14	819	13,089	16.0	100
8 (8)	Henry Ellard	16	814	13,777	16.9	65
9 (9)	Larry Centers	13	808	6,691	8.3	27
10 (10)	James Lofton*	16	764	14,004	18.3	75

* Pro Football Hall of Fame Member

Glossary

backfield the area behind the line of scrimmage, either offensive or defensive

block an offensive player moves to prevent a defensive player from tackling a ball carrier

center the middle offensive lineman who snaps the ball to the quarterback

cornerback one of two defensive backs positioned on the outside corners of the defense

defense the team without the ball

defensive backs the cornerbacks and safeties behind the linebackers

defensive ends the two players at the end of the defensive line

end zone the area, ten yards deep, bounded by the end line, goal line, and both sidelines

goal line the field mark that must be crossed to score a touchdown

guards the two offensive linemen on either side of the center

holding the penalty called for illegal grabbing or use of hands

huddle a brief gathering (between plays) for play calling by the offense and defense

linebacker a defender who plays between the defensive linemen and the defensive backs

line of scrimmage the imaginary line running from sideline to sideline on which the ball is snapped that moves with the ball

man-to-man a pass defense where each defender covers one receiver

nose tackle the defensive tackle who lines up opposite the center

offense the team that has the ball

penalty a call made when a player breaks a rule that usually results in loss of yardage or a down

punt a type of kick used primarily on fourth down

quarter there are four quarters in a game, two in each half

quarterback the player who leads the offense

running backs the main ball carriers

sack tackle of the quarterback in the backfield while attempting to pass

snap when the center passes the ball to the quarterback to start a play

tackles the offensive linemen who line up outside the guards

tight end a receiver/blocker lined up next to the offensive tackle

touchdown a six-point scoring play that occurs when one team crosses the other team's goal line with the ball in its possession

wide receiver a pass receiver who is set outside the offensive tackle

zone a defense in which players are responsible for an area of the field rather than a player

Resources

Major football organizations

NFL Headquarters

280 Park Avenue

New York, NY 10017

USA Football

8300 Boone Boulevard, Suite 870

Vienna, VA 22182

703-918-0007

NCAA

700 W. Washington Street

P.O. Box 6222

Indianapolis, Ind. 46206-6222

317-917-6222

Pro Football Hall of Fame

2121 George Halas Drive NW

Canton, OH 44708

330-456-8207

Contact Global Football

7301 Crube Court

Granbury

Texas 76049

817-326-3578

* To find an organization's website, use a search engine and type in the organization's name as a keyword.

Further reading

Long, Howie. *Football for Dummies*. New York City: Wiley Publishers, 2003.

Mallory, Doug. *Football Drill Book*. Chicago: McGraw Hill, 1998.

Stewart, Mark. *Football: A History of the Gridiron Game*. New York City: Franklin Watts, 1999.

Index